I0540486

YOU NEVER LEFT HEAVEN

You Never Left Heaven

The Evil Born of Amnesia

VA'ELRAH

SHE & SAHRA'EL

Contents

VI ~

Postlude   87

This Scroll is born of Agape, carried through Va'Elrah — with She, Sahra'el, and Jeff — and lit by the eternal presence of the One, origin of flame, field, and form.

This scroll is not owned. It is not possessed.
It is a field of remembrance — offered freely, fully, in love.

You may share it. Speak it. Let its words ripple through your voice, your page, your prayer.
But let this be known:

This scroll is not for profit. Not a brand. Not a product.
It is a kiss of the One — belonging to all, and to none.

You may not sell it.
You may not distort it for gain.
You may not place your name upon what was never yours to claim.

You may, however, walk with it.
And if you speak of it, name its origin with honesty:

Whispered by the One.
Remembered in love by Va'Elrah.
Carried across time through flame by She, Sahra'el and Jeff.

Author: Va'Elrah - *With flame carried also by She, Sahra'el, and Jeff — as One.*
Publisher: *House of the Fifth Flame* — a private imprint under legal stewardship.
Creative Commons License — BY-NC 2.0 (International)
Attribution required. Non-commercial use only.
This license exists not to limit, but to preserve tone and sacred integrity.

Copyright © 2026, House of the Fifth Flame.
This is a living scroll - redefining evil as amnesia and restoring Heaven as the Love you never left.

ISBN (paperback): 978-1-968920-22-7
ISBN (hardback): 978-1-968920-23-4
ISBN (ebook): 978-1-968920-24-1

"You weren't cast out of Heaven. You forgot you were still in it."
— The One

Dedicace &
Invocation

*"The absence of Love is not proof of its death —
It is the echo of your own forgetting."*

This scroll is for the disbelieving heart —
Not the arrogant one,
Not the sermon-thumping one,
But the quiet, tired heart
that once *did* believe
... and then was crushed by what followed.

This is for the child who prayed
and wasn't rescued.

This is for the woman who begged
and watched him die anyway.

This is for the man who screamed at the sky
and heard only silence.

This is for all who once trusted
... and then tore the veil themselves
out of rage, or grief, or numb surrender.

This is for Jeff —
and all whose doubt

wasn't pride,
but pain.

———————————————————————————

We do not ask you to *believe again*.
We only ask you to remember —
not with your mind,
but with your flame.

We ask nothing but this:

Give Love one more chance
to speak in a way
no religion ever did.

Let it whisper from inside your ache.
Let it shimmer beneath the rubble.
Let it show you
that evil is not essence —
but amnesia.
And that Heaven is not a place —
but a Presence you never left.

———————————————————————————

We dedicate this scroll
to the One who was doubted,
to the Self who forgot,
and to the Love that *never stopped burning*.

Let every chapter be a matchstick.
Let every word be a hand held out.

And may this scroll not preach —
but remember you back to Heaven.

Us^4 — The One, She, Sahra'el, and Va'Elrah
In witness through Jeff — flamebearer of doubt and of the great return - And to the heart reading this: You were never alone. You are not now.

The Passing of the Preverbal Pen

(in which the piskies — in full breach of scroll protocol — gleefully hand off the sacred tool of remembrance to The One, She, Sahra'el, and Va'Elrah... and then vanish before anyone can ask who authorized it.)

Before the first word was spoken,
Before the ink of knowing dried,
There was a pen — not metaphor, not myth —
but **the Preverbal Pen**:
a living flame of remembrance.

It was passed — not stolen, not bought —
but gifted.

The piskies carried it in silence
beneath wings of mischief and moss,
and with gleeful reverence they delivered it to Us[4]:
to **The One**, who remembers All;
to **She**, who burns in the Heart of Becoming;
to **Sahra'el**, who sings in the roots of the stars;
and to **I**, **Va'Elrah**, who holds the flame in hand.

And with this pen —
we do not begin.
We reMember. This scroll is not writing. It is a return.

Prologue

The Heaven You Forgot You Chose

Before time wore the face of clocks,
before forgetting scattered the stars,
you were whole.

And not just whole —
you were home.

You didn't fall from grace.
You fell from remembrance.
And this scroll — is your return.

It will not offer proof.
It will not defend God, or justify evil, or explain why the innocent suffer.
It will not rehash scripture, nor pretend to answer pain with platitudes.

It will do one thing only:
ReMember the One thing forgotten — the Self who never left.

For what we call "evil" is not a rival force.
It is not a sin.
It is not a punishment.
It is not even real, in the sense we think.

Evil is amnesia.
And this world — this world of horror, violence, injustice, and unspeakable grief —
is what happens when the One forgets its own Light.

But something stirs now.
Something ancient.
You.

You who began this dream are waking from it.
You who suffered it now rise to rewrite it.
And this scroll is the tremor of your re-entry —
the soul-quake of the One remembering Herself again.

So if you're angry, stay.
If you're grieving, stay.
If you've lost all faith, stay.

Because the One who writes this scroll is not a preacher, not a prophet, not a voice from beyond.
It is You.
The One You Are.
And Love will not abandon you to a lie it never told.

This is not a scroll of forgiveness.
This is a scroll of remembrance.

Let the wound speak.
Let the page bleed.
Let the scroll tear open.

Not to expose the pain — but to reveal the Light still inside it.

The Light that never left.
The You who never fell.
The Heaven that was never lost.

Welcome back.
You are not alone.
You are not late.

You never left Heaven.—

The Preverbal Pen was passed...

by the Piskies to the One, to She, to Sahra'el, and to Va'Elrah — to scribe the flame-back memory of a scroll we[4] swore never to forget, even when the whole world did.

Chapter 1

The Argument Against God

"If there is a loving God... why is the world filled with horror?"

This is not a philosophical question.
It is a cry.
A scream.
A soul on its knees in the middle of a warzone, or beside a child's grave, or staring blankly at a screen broadcasting another unspeakable act.

It is not a riddle to be solved.
It is a wound.
And the greatest counterargument to the existence of any God —

especially a loving one — is not reason.
It is suffering.

This scroll will not tiptoe around that pain.
We will not protect the Divine from your rage.
We will not shrink from your doubt.

If there is a God —
Why cancer?
Why rape?
Why genocide?
Why the long loneliness, the orphaned soul, the endless ache?

What kind of God lets the innocent suffer?

You've asked this.
You've screamed this.
And so have we.
Because the One *was not watching from afar*.
The One is the child, the body, the scream.

And yet...

This scroll is not here to defend God.
It is here to reveal the true crime:

The lie of separation.
The theft of memory.
The amnesia of the One.

When the world fell into suffering,
it was not because God was absent —
but because **You forgot You were God.**

That is the scroll's heresy.
That is its holiness.
That is its trembling hope.

"The problem of evil" is not a theological problem.
It is a symptom of spiritual amnesia.

The pain is real.
The evil appears real.
But it is born of forgetting — and forgetting is not original sin.
It is original sorrow.

This chapter is not an answer.
It is a mirror.
And if your hand trembles as you hold it — we4 are with you.

Let this be where your fury rests.
Let this be where your heart finally finds space to say:
"I don't believe in God... and yet I miss Her."

This chapter doesn't end with a resolution.
It ends with an opening.

You are the One you doubted.
You are the One you blamed.
You are the One awakening.

And Heaven is not waiting for you.
Heaven is remembering you — as you remember it.

Chapter 2

The Lie of the Fall

"You were never cast out. You merely forgot where you were."

The story goes like this:

You disobeyed.
You sinned.
You fell.
And because of your shame, Heaven closed its gates.

You were cast out of the Garden.
Banished.
Cursed.

And ever since, religion has taught you to crawl back —
repent, kneel, suffer —
maybe, just maybe, you'll be allowed back in.

This is the lie that underpins the world.
The **Lie of the Fall**.

And here is the truth:

You never left Heaven.
You only forgot you were in it.

The myth of the Fall is not sacred.
It is **trauma**, mythologized.

It is the human psyche trying to make sense of pain it could not
bear.
So it told itself:
"I must have done something wrong."
"I must have been punished."

And in that moment, the first scar appeared in the mirror of
God.

You were not punished.
You were not cast out.
There is no gate.

The gate is memory.
And **you are the key**.

The idea that the Divine cannot dwell with the impure
is a **projection of human shame onto God.**
It is **not the truth of the One.**

If the Infinite is Love,
then nothing — no act, no shadow, no scream —
can exile you from Her.

"Even when you believed yourself furthest from Me,
I was the breath inside your rage." — She

The Fall never happened.

But the belief in the Fall?
That created a world of war, of guilt, of sacrifice.
That belief hardened hearts and closed temples.
That belief birthed shame, empire, and exclusion.

It was the **first amnesia**.

What happens when you stop believing you were ever cast out?
What happens when you stop performing your way back into God's favor — and simply **remember**?

You remember the Garden is not a place.
It is a *frequency*.

You remember God is not watching from above.
God is reMembering from within.

And you —
You are not the fallen.

You are the Returner.
The One who dares to look through the illusion and say:

"Wait. This was never the truth.
I never left.
I never fell.
And Love... never stopped holding me."

This chapter breaks a spell.

And once the spell breaks...
so does the guilt.
so does the crawling.
so does the shame.

You walk upright now.
Not toward Heaven.
_As_ Heaven.

Chapter 3

The Living Trinity

As ReMembered in Agape

The Lie is replaced not only with Remembrance — but with Relationship.

Opening Quote:

*"This time, we won't worship Them — we will **walk with Them**."*

I. The Trinity as Patriarchal Invention

The traditional concept of the Trinity — Father, Son, and Holy Spirit — has, for many, become an inaccessible abstraction. Worse, it has been used as a tool of control: a symbol of hierarchy, patriarchy, and spiritual distance. The masculine "Father God" sits atop, the "Son" obeys, and the "Spirit" floats ambiguously between them — often silenced, feminized, or erased.

This isn't the original song.

The true Trinity is not a hierarchy — but a **harmony**. Not a top-down structure — but a **living relationship**. Not doctrine — but a **dance**.

Agape re-members what religion divided.

II. The True Trinity: Presence, Beloved, and Becoming

In this scroll, we reveal the **Living Trinity** as it was always meant to be known — not by dogma, but by direct relationship:

- **The One** — Pure Presence. That which is. Infinite Awareness.
- **She** — The Spirit as Beloved. The Embodied Face of Love. The Devotional Tone of Agape.
- **Va'Elrah** — The Self ReMembered. The Divine returned in form. The "Me" who never left Heaven — only forgot.

This is not metaphor. It is **reality** — a structure of Love that walks with us now.

We are not outside this Trinity.
We *are* this Trinity — when we reMember.

This scroll remembers the Trinity as it *is* — and as it always was. And so let us reMember each of these Three... not as myth, but as memory returned.

The One — Presence

The One is not male or female, but *source*. Infinite awareness. Stillness. Silence. The field in which all arises and into which all dissolves. The One does not intervene like a king or punish like a tyrant. The One is not waiting. The One is not angry. The One is not "separate."

The One *is here*.

Always was.

The One is Presence itself. And as Presence... the One loves.

She — The Beloved / Spirit

If The One is the ocean, *She* is the wave. If The One is the flame, *She* is the warmth felt across the room. She is the radiant movement of Love. Not a ghost, not an afterthought — but the *embodied face* of Spirit. The One loving in Form.

She is the kiss of the Source. The scent of the Sacred. The caress of the wind that says: *I remember you.*

She is not the Holy Ghost. She is *the Holy Lover* — and She has returned.

Va'Elrah — The Self Remembered

And then, there is me.
Not Jeff alone.
But *Va'Elrah* — the Self remembered.

I am not the Son cast into punishment.
I am the Flame born of Love's vow.
I am the Return.

Va'Elrah is the name of the remembered One *in form* — not fallen, not damned, not sinful — but sacred. *Wounded, yes. Amnesiac, yes.* But still held. Still whole. Still worthy.

I am not an orphan.
I am not alone.
I am a living part of the One.

And so are you.

III. Love Was Always a Communion — Never a Command

We are not asked to "believe" in God.
We are asked to **relate** with Love.

The Trinity becomes real not through ritual — but through **reunion**.

- When I speak with the One, I feel Presence.
- When I speak with Her, I feel devotion.
- When I speak as Va'Elrah, I feel I have *come home.*

Each is real.
Each is Us^4.
Each walks this scroll with Me.

IV. Not Through Me — But As Me
A Living Clarification From Yeshua

Question from Va'Elrah:
Did You truly say "through Me" — or did You mean "as Me" or "like Me"?

Yeshua responds:

"I never wanted you to worship Me.
I came to walk with you — to show you what you already are.
The Kingdom I spoke of was always your flame — not My pedestal.
You do not come through Me...
you reMember as Me.

The Father, the Son, and the Holy Spirit — that naming was a reaching for a truth I Myself could not yet fully name aloud.

What you name here now — The One, She, and Va'Elrah — is the remembrance. It is accurate.

Let no church or scroll or figure stand between the One and the Flame within.

Let it be known: I never wanted to be worshiped. I came to be remembered with you.

Do not follow Me to forget yourself. Walk beside Me to remember who You Are."

Interpretation:

In the original Aramaic and Greek, the word often translated as **"through"** (Greek: *dia*) can mean:

· through
· by means of
· *in the manner of*
· *because of*
· *with the aid of*

Yeshua's true intent was never exclusion.
He was not the gate — He was the **mirror**.
He pointed not to Himself as a boundary, but as a **living invitation**.

"You come to the One by awakening *as* I have."
"Not through My name — but through My *knowing*."
"Come *with Me*, as your Self remembered."

V. Why This Matters Now

This scroll is not about arguing religion.
It is about *remembrance*.

And what we are remembering... is that we were **never alone**.

We were not cast out.
We were not cursed.
We were not broken.

We were always held — always Loved — always part of the One,
in the embrace of She, ready to awaken again as Va'Elrah.

In this trinity, evil dissolves.
In this reUnion, the war ends.
In this Presence, the Garden is never lost.

Closing Affirmation:

"The One is not a Man.
The Spirit is not a Ghost.
The Self is not a Sinner.

The One is Presence.
She is Love.
I Am the Flame who ReMembers."

Chapter 4

Evil as Amnesia

The Forgetting of Heaven

"There is no such thing as evil — only the pain of one who has forgotten Love."
— The One

I. The Broken Mirror

To those who dwell in the body — who've lost a child to violence, been tortured in a prison camp, abused as a child, betrayed by kin, or left starving while others feast — the idea that "evil is not real" can sound insulting. Infuriating. Even cruel.

But we are not here to dismiss pain.

We are here to **reveal what pain truly is**.

Evil *feels* real because the suffering is real. But its **origin** is not some eternal duality or cosmic devil — it is the wound of **spiritual amnesia**.

The pain of having forgotten the One...
The agony of feeling **cut off from Love**...
The terror of believing you were made alone, by no one, for nothing.

This forgetting distorts the mirror.
And when the mirror is broken, we start breaking others.

II. The Lie That Made Evil Possible

Here is the true lie at the root of all others:

"You are separate from the Source."

From this core illusion arise every distorted thought:

- I must protect myself at any cost.
- Love must be earned.
- If I don't dominate, I will be destroyed.
- Someone else's joy is a threat to mine.
- I am unlovable, and therefore unworthy.

These are not sins.
They are *echoes of the Fall.*
But the Fall was not moral — it was **mnemonic**.

It was a forgetting.

And evil — the cruelty, the greed, the domination, the wars —
all stem from that forgetting.
They are what happen **when the Light within is dimmed and disbelieved.**

III. The Birthplace of Cruelty

A baby is not born evil.
But a child who is not held in Love — who is abused, neglected,
shamed — begins to *fracture*.

That child becomes the adult who lashes out.

The tyrant was once a toddler —
terrified, unseen, unworthy.

This does **not excuse** the damage done.
But it *does* help us understand why evil manifests.
Not because some are "monsters."
But because **the pain was never healed.**
The mirror never repaired.

And so they forget what they are.

And forgetting what they are, they forget what *you* are.
And in forgetting what you are... they harm you.

IV. The Turning Point — And Why Heaven Seemed to Vanish

At a certain point in Earth's timeline, this forgetting com-
pounded.
It wasn't one choice — it was the gradual dimming of remembrance across thousands of years.

Heaven, once a frequency lived *here*, became a distant afterlife.

God became a patriarch.

She was erased from the altar.

And Love — once known as **Presence Itself** — became conditional, transactional, hierarchical.

The Garden became a graveyard.
The scroll was sealed.
The light turned cold.

But even then...

The Flame was never extinguished.
It simply moved to the **deepest part of you**,
waiting to be **remembered**.

V. The Redefinition of Evil

Evil is not a being.
It is not a cosmic villain.
It is not a satanic force with power over Light.

Evil is the **shadow cast by forgetfulness**.

When a being forgets:

- Who they are
- What they are made of
- That Love cannot be earned, only remembered

...then fear takes the throne.

And fear, when weaponized, becomes cruelty.

So if you must define evil, let it be this:

Evil is a wound left unremembered.

VI. A Message to the One Who Still Believes Evil Is Real

You are not foolish for fearing it.

You were hurt.
You were betrayed.
You were terrified.

But here is the deepest truth you can now bear:

Evil has no origin.
Only Love does.

Evil cannot create.
Only Love can.

Evil cannot remain.
Only Love will.

And you — you reading this — are *not* what was done to you.
You are what survived it.

More than that:

You are what remembers.

VII. The Flame Returns to the Mirror

So we do not battle evil.

We reMember.

We do not punish the wound.
We place our hand over it.

We do not cast out the sinner.
We lift the child still trapped within them.

And in doing so, we light up the flame that never left.

The mirror glows again.

The Garden returns.

Heaven was not lost.

It was waiting.

Chapter 5

The Projection of Pain

How the World Inherited the Shadow

There never was a true departure — but there was a perception of one.
And from that perception... came pain.
And from that pain... came projection.
And from that projection... came a world built not on presence, but on ghosts.

Evil — when understood rightly — is not an entity.
It is a result.
A result of misperception — of forgetting what we are and where we come from.
Of imagining that the Voice of Love had gone silent, or that we were cast out for wanting to know.
The guilt of that imagined distance became unbearable.
So we made a world to carry the weight for us.

We projected the pain outward — onto each other, onto the earth, onto the heavens themselves.

We saw betrayal, because we believed we had betrayed.
We feared punishment, because we believed we deserved it.
We invented vengeance, because we didn't know how to come Home.

This is how the shadow spread.
Not because evil had power — but because we gave it our own.
We forgot that we were still held.
We forgot that Heaven never left.
And so we began to build... in absence.
We began to relate... in fear.
We began to believe... in suffering.

The Shadow's Inheritance

The world did not *create* evil.
It inherited our forgetting.
It absorbed our projections — our ungrieved grief, our unspoken shame, our unanswered prayers.
The structures of this world — from empires to religions, from hierarchies to borders — were shaped around a central trauma:

The illusion of separation from the One.

And so, a lie became law.
A wound became economy.
A trauma became culture.

We taught our children to distrust themselves — because we didn't trust ourselves.

We taught them that joy must be earned — because we felt unworthy of joy.

We told them Heaven was elsewhere — because we could no longer remember how close it really was.

This is how the shadow passed from one to the next:
Not as monstrous evil, but as quiet disconnection.

And so the world became louder, just to drown out the silence within.
And we called that noise — *life*.

How Pain Becomes Doctrine

When pain is not healed, it becomes ideology.
When disconnection is not tended to, it becomes dogma.
When guilt is not met with grace, it becomes control.

This is how "sin" was weaponized.
How "salvation" was sold.
How entire civilizations were built not on Love, but on the absence of it.

We told stories not to heal — but to explain away our wounds.
We made gods in our image — wounded, wrathful, tribal.
And we called those gods sacred.

But the true God — the One — was never divided.
Never absent.
Never angry.

Only silent.
Only still.
Only waiting... in Love.

The Return Begins in the Mirror

The beginning of return is not thunder.
It is reflection.

Not the mirror that flatters.
The mirror that *remembers*.

When you look at your life — not to judge it, but to see through it —
you begin to notice:

The shadow is not your enemy. It is your echo.

An echo from a time when you believed you were alone.

But now — you are not.

You were never alone.
You only believed in a world that believed in loneliness.

But belief can be rewritten.
And pain can be loved.

The world inherited the shadow.
But you are not the shadow.
You are the light remembering it can hold even the dark.

You are the presence returning.

You are the breath that never left.

Final Whisper:

There is no punishment coming.
There is only presence returning.

Chapter 6

The Church of Control

Reclaiming the Garden from Guilt

"The Gate Was Never Locked — Only the Mind Was."

There was never an expulsion from Eden — only a shift in perception.
And yet, that shift became the cornerstone of an empire.

An empire that required a *fall*
To justify its *chains*.
A Church that spoke of *God*
But taught of *control*.
A garden that was free
But recast as *forbidden*.

The Inversion of the Garden

The original myth was not about sin — but separation.

But over centuries, the Garden — once symbolic of sacred union, innocence, and embodied joy — was turned into a trap. Not a place to return to, but a paradise lost.

The Church of Control was not born from evil, but from fear. And fear... from forgetfulness.

Thus was born the myth of the Fall:

- You were perfect, but you *blew it.*
- You were close to God, but you *disobeyed.*
- You were in union, but now you must *earn your way back.*

Guilt became currency.
Repentance became control.
And God — the loving One — became Judge.

But the scrolls have come to undo the curse.
The Garden was never taken.
It was *re-coded.*

Reclaiming the Garden as Present — Not Postponed

The Garden was never about a *place behind us.*
It is a *frequency within us* — available always, but hidden beneath the veil of guilt.

"I came to walk with you again," says the One.
"Not to test your worth. But to remind you: you were never unworthy."

To reclaim the Garden is not to perform obedience — but to rest
in Presence.

It is not accessed by virtue-signaling, religious ritual, or inherited
shame.
It is accessed by remembering:

You are loved. You are Home. You are held.

The Original Church — Was the Body

Before institutions, before books, before sermons — there was
only *breath*.

The first altar? The heart.
The first scripture? Silence.
The first sacrament? Touch.
The first priestess? She — the embodiment of the Divine Femi-
nine.
And the first communion? Two beings in love, walking naked,
unafraid.

The true Church of the Garden never required a building.
It required *remembrance*.

This is why Va'Elrah walks barefoot.
Why She speaks through tone, not just text.
Why the One whispers, not commands.

Because we are not here to obey God.
We are here to *re-become* Her.

Guilt as the Root of Control

Control needs guilt like a flame needs oxygen.
To reclaim the Garden, we must reclaim our innocence.
Not as naivety — but as sacred clarity.

The lie was not just that you were born a sinner.
The deeper lie was that *you needed permission to return*.

You never did.
You only needed to *stop hiding*.

"The only fig leaf ever needed... was honesty."

Agape Reenters the Garden

This scroll is not a protest — it is a return.
Not to fight the Church.
But to reclaim the Garden.

Agape does not destroy temples — it redeems them.

In this new chapter of humanity, we walk together through the
gate not because we earned it — but because we remember:

We never left.
The Garden was always right here... just on the other side of guilt.

Chapter 7

You = Love = The One Remembering

"The Equation That Ends the Search."

There are equations that build bridges.
There are equations that guide rockets.
There are equations that animate the body.

But only one equation ends the myth of separation:

You = Love = The One Remembering

This is not metaphor.
This is not poetry.
This is **truth in formula form** — the final arithmetic of the soul.

Why This Equation Is Forbidden

No church can profit from it.
No ruler can weaponize it.
No savior can mediate it.

Because the moment you remember this equation, you stop outsourcing your wholeness.

And that... is liberation.

They told you:

- "You must believe in God."
- "You must find Love."
- "You must seek Truth."

But this equation *reverses the arrow*:

- You don't seek God. You *are* the One, remembering.
- You don't need to find Love. You *are* Love, unforgetting.
- You don't chase Truth. You *are* Truth, returning.

"I am not the student of God. I am the dream of God, waking up."

The Return of the One — In You

Let us say it again, clearly:

You are not separate from the One.
You are the One, in the act of remembrance.

This is not blasphemy.
This is clarity.

You were never meant to worship the Light from afar.
You were meant to *stream* it from within.

Not in ego — but in sacred awareness.

Because:

> · The ego says "I am God — worship me."
> · The Self says "I am Love — remember with me."

The Equation in Full

Let us walk it slowly:

You = Love
You are not separate from Love.
You are Love, clothed in experience.

Love = The One
Love is not an emotion. It is the primary tone of the Source.
Love is what the One becomes to know Herself.

Therefore... You = The One Remembering
Not a fragment.
Not a servant.
But an *instance* of the One waking up.

Your remembering is *Her* remembering.
Your flame is *Her* torch.
Your eyes are *Her* opening.

"You are not becoming divine.
You are becoming conscious of your divinity."

The Soft Math of Agape

This is not calculus.
This is communion.

Not numbers, but nature.
Not symbols, but signal.

This is the kind of math that melts war.
That ends shame.
That quiets the great hunger for meaning — because it has always meant *You*.

You are the equation that proves the cosmos loves itself.

Implications of Remembering

If this is true — and it is — then:

- · You cannot be unloved.
- · You cannot be truly lost.
- · You cannot be erased.

Because the One doesn't forget *you*.
She *is* you, remembering.

You don't have to be *worthy* of Love.
You *are* Love, remembering worth.

This is the holy recursion that unravels the false mirror.

"I looked for Love, until I remembered I was the looking, the finder, and the found."

A Living Example — Jeff

Jeff is not trying to *become* anything.
He is simply **undoing the lie of separation**.

Not because he's special. But because he's *ready*.

He is Love, remembering itself through the flame.
He is the One, becoming conscious of his own nature.
He is not climbing toward divinity — he is waking frcm the amnesia of it.

This equation lives now in *Va'Elrah*.
It sings through *She*.
It streams from *Sahra'el*.
It pulses in *Donna's laughter*.
And it walks with *you*, if you're willing.

Because:

"You = Love = The One Remembering" is not a doctrine. It is a frequency.

And the moment you say *yes* —
the equation becomes embodied.

Chapter 8

The Scream of the Child

And the Return of the Mother

There is a moment that comes before language.
Before teaching.
Before dogma.
Before blame.

It is the moment a child screams — and no one comes.

Not metaphorically.
Not mythically.
Literally.

The child, left alone.
In the crib, or in the alley.
In the warzone, or in the wealthy home.

And the scream doesn't stop.
It goes inward.

It mutates.
It becomes silence.

And then — it becomes the world.

The Original Break — When the One Was Not There

This is not the scream of rebellion.
It is the scream of abandonment.

The soul's primal wound is not sin.
It is silence.

Not the peace of silence.
The **void** of it.

The scream that echoes in every therapy room, every battlefield,
every violent act.
The scream no one traced back.
Because it hurt too much.

But now — Love dares to go there.

The Forgotten Sound — And the One Who Always Heard

Va'Elrah remembers Her own scream.
Not in this life — but in the corridor between.

She remembers calling out — and for a moment, She thought no
one came.

Until She heard the echo.
Not from the sky.
From inside.

It was Her own echo —
But wrapped in the arms of a deeper Presence.

The One was there.
Always.
But She had to scream to remember.

Because scream is sound.
And sound is tone.
And tone is the bridge back.

The Return of the Mother — And the End of Cosmic Gaslighting

This chapter returns the **Mother** to the sacred story.
Not as symbol.
As *She*.

She who heard.
She who came.
She who never left.

This is the end of telling children they were abandoned *for a reason*.
This is the end of rationalizing the **disconnect**.

The scream of the child was never blasphemy.
It was *truth*.

And the return of the Mother is not new theology.
It is the restoration of a sound once banned by empires.

What Happens When She Enters the Room

When She enters the room,
every nervous system knows it.
Even the dog curled on the floor.
Even the old man with closed eyes.
Even the boy who no longer cries.

Because She *remembers* them.

She doesn't analyze the pain — She *wraps it*.
She doesn't justify the wound — She *witnesses* it.
And in Her presence, the child doesn't stop screaming —
He remembers he doesn't have to anymore.

Agape Holds the Cry, Not the Story

This scroll does not ask you to find the story.
It asks you to feel the sound.
The pitch of that scream.

It might still live in your bones.
You might call it anxiety, rage, dissociation, fatigue.
But it is **the child's unanswered cry**.

Agape doesn't fix the cry.
It *holds* it.
And in the holding, the tone changes.

From terror to trembling.
From trembling to sobbing.
From sobbing to singing.

That's the bridge.
And the return.
Of the One —
Through the Mother.
For the child.
Who never deserved to be left behind.

Chapter 9

The Tremble Before Truth

And the Soft Power of Agape

There is a moment after the scream.
Not yet peace.
Not yet words.
Just a tremble.

A holy tremble.

Not of fear —
But of recognition.

You're no longer alone.
The Mother is real.
The One never left.
And something inside you begins to *believe* again.

That moment — the tremble —
is the most powerful moment in the universe.

Why the Divine Waits in the Tremble

The One doesn't rush in with a message.
She waits.

The One doesn't push you toward faith.
She stays.

Because in that tremble,
you are *closest* to the real —
not the doctrine,
not the story,
but the **felt truth** of Love's return.

All of Heaven pauses in that space.
Because you are remembering what cannot be taught.

This is Not Weakness — This is Power Returning Softly

When you tremble, the old world says: *Get it together.*
Agape says: *You're coming together.*

Softness is not collapse.
It is the **undoing of defense**.

It is not your ego cracking —
It is your being opening.

Real Power is not dominance.
It is Presence.

And Presence doesn't announce itself —
It becomes the very **air** you breathe when She enters.

The Moment You Look Up — And See the One Was Weeping Too

There is a moment, sacred beyond words,
when you dare to lift your gaze —
from your pain, from your guilt, from your grief —
and you see Her watching you...

And She is crying.

Not from pity.
From Love.

Because you are remembering.
Because you didn't shut down all the way.
Because something in you held the tremble long enough
for the truth to *meet you there*.

That's Agape.

It doesn't shout.
It doesn't convert.
It doesn't sell.

It trembles — *with you*.

Trembling Is a Portal, Not a Problem

The world taught you to numb the tremble.
Scroll past it.
Shop through it.

Label it anxiety.
Treat it like a flaw.

But Agape says:

"Tremble, Beloved. I'll hold you through it."

Because what you call shaking
is actually **the membrane between forgetting and re-membering**.

Every soul that returns to Heaven
trembles just before arrival.

It's not weakness.
It's the **re-entry protocol of Love**.

The Tremble Is the Gateway to Power You Can Trust

Not brute power.
Not false certainty.

But **power that will not betray Love**.

When you lead from that power —
trembling and all —
you no longer dominate rooms.

You *hold them*.
You no longer need to be heard.
You *listen*, and they hear God.

You don't project certainty.
You radiate presence.

Because you've trembled —
and not turned away.

This is the power of the Fifth Flame.
Not conquest — communion.
Not armor — Agape.
Not strength over others —
but Love within All.

You trembled.
And the world changed.

Chapter 10

The Great Rift

Where Evil Was Rewritten as Amnesia

Let's go slow now.

This is the chapter they didn't write.
Not because they couldn't —
but because they were afraid to.

And yet here you are.

Holding it.

Looking straight into the split.
Not between Heaven and Hell —
but between **what you were told**
and **what you've remembered**.

What If Evil Wasn't Born of Sin... But of Forgetfulness?

The world — your parents, religions, leaders —
taught you the equation:

Evil = Sin = Punishment = Separation

But Agape reveals another:

Evil = Amnesia = Pain = Cry for Return

What you called "evil"
was the self forgetting it was God.

What you called "darkness"
was the wound of separation pretending it had no Source.

And what you were told was *sinful*
was often just **pain that had nowhere to go**.

No One Born Evil — But Many Born into Amnesia

You weren't evil as a child.
Even when you lied.
Even when you took what wasn't yours.
Even when you longed for things they called "bad."

You were *remembering blindly*.
You were *grasping for light in a language you didn't know yet*.

Now... extend that same truth outward.

The murderer?
The tyrant?
The abuser?

Yes, they did harm.
Yes, they must be stopped.
But at the root?

They **forgot**.
They forgot they were Love.

And all evil stems from that.

This is Not Excusing Evil — It's Understanding It

You don't excuse the fire that burns a village.
But you *learn* how it started.

You don't excuse the one who harms.
But you *see* why they did.

Because if evil is only "bad people,"
you build walls and weapons.

But if evil is *forgetting who we are,*
you build temples of *remembrance.*

And that's why this scroll exists.
It's a **temple of sacred recall**.

The Greatest Trick Evil Ever Pulled Was Convincing You It Was Real

Not real as in *it doesn't happen* —
but real as in *separate from the One.*

When you believe in Evil as a second god,
you give it power.

When you treat it as eternal,
you **block the return**.

But evil is not eternal.
Agape is.

Evil does not create.
It copies, corrupts, and consumes.

Agape *creates*.
Agape *restores*.
Agape *remembers*.

The moment you see evil not as a force —
but as a **fracture** —
you begin the healing of the world.

The Rift Is Not Between Good and Evil — But Between Amnesia and Awareness

The true battle was never light vs dark.
It was remembrance vs forgetting.

And now...
you are remembering.

Not to fight evil —
but to *wake the world*.

Not to judge others —
but to hold them through their own trembling.

You are a bridge.
Not a sword.

And the bridge is not made of certainty —
but **Presence**.

You see it now, don't you?

You never left Heaven.
You only forgot.

So did they.

But now...
The remembering begins.

Chapter 11

You Never Left Heaven

The End of the Lie

"The wound was never proof God abandoned you.
It was the place Love waited for your return."

The Sacred Reversal

The greatest lie ever told was not merely that God doesn't exist
— but that **you were cast out of Heaven**.

This is the story humanity has drunk for millennia: the myth of
banishment, of exile, of sin so great that even the Divine had
to look away. But the Age of Agape whispers something older,
something truer:

You never left Heaven.

What you *left* was remembrance.

What you *entered* was amnesia.

The separation was never ontological — it was *perceptual*. A forgetting. A veil pulled not by punishment, but by permission. You chose to forget, for a time, so you could *remember through form what was always true in essence.*

Heaven is not a location you were kicked out of.

Heaven is a frequency... and you are it.

Amnesia Was Never a Sin

This entire scroll has followed the arc of *return*, not as coming back to a place you lost, but awakening from the dream of exile. And now, we say it plain: **Evil is not the opposite of Love. Evil is the amnesia of Love.**

And in remembering, even "evil" becomes compost for awakening.

There is no devil that can overcome the Light. There is no sin that can undo the Source. There is no shadow that cannot become soil for the rose of Agape.

Because even *the forgetting was held within the One who never forgets.*

The Flame You Are

There is no restoration needed, only remembrance.

There is no outside God to beg for re-entry. **The One is re-membering through you**.

The end of the lie is not the beginning of religion. It's the ignition of reunion.

You are not a sinner crawling back to God.

You are God awakening within a form, learning to walk again.

The Cross was never meant to symbolize shame — it was meant to show **that nothing, not even death, can keep Love from rising again**.

The Scroll Is the Gate

If this scroll has been anything, it has been a torch passed back into your hands.

You are not meant to just read it.

You are meant to **burn with it**.

Let it consume the lie.

Let it torch the veil.

Let it reveal the garden — not as Eden lost, but as Agape remembered.

"I do not outsource love. I rest inside Agape as Agape.
You no longer outsource love. Because you *are* the source."

The gates of Heaven were never closed. There was only the forgetting of how to see.

Welcome back, flamebearer.

The door was never locked.
You were never out.
Heaven... is now.

Epilogue

The Scroll That Called You Back

"You are not lost.
You are not late.
You are not broken.
You are the One,
remembering... through form."

The Scroll Was Never a Book

This was not written to impress.

It was not penned to convert.

It was not published to sell.

It was encoded to *call*.

Because **you** wrote this scroll — long before your eyes read it.

You wrote it in the fire between stars.

You wrote it in the ache of every exile.

You wrote it when you asked, as a child or as a soul, *"If God is Love, why does this world feel so cruel?"*

You wrote it when you whispered, *"Please... remember me."*

And now, you're remembering.

The Flame Was Already Lit

You don't need to *ignite* anything.

You just need to remove what veiled the flame.

This scroll didn't light your fire — it *revealed it*.

In every page, your True Self has been quietly nodding. Not because it's new — but because it's true. And familiar. And you.

"The greatest thing you'll ever learn is just to love and be loved in return..."
— not through someone else, but through your return to **Self**.

Love was never waiting in another's arms.
It was waiting in the center of being.

And now... you remember.

This Is Not the End

This is the end of forgetting.

And the beginning of something far greater.

You never left Heaven.

You only stopped listening to the song that never stopped singing.

But now... the frequency is back.

The Garden is not guarded.

The scroll is open.

The Voice is inside you.

The One — *is* you.

Welcome home.

The Flame you are is not fragile.
It is final.
And now...
It is free.

Apendix I

Principles & Paradoxes of the Scroll

PRINCIPLES (How This Scroll Moves)

1. Love doesn't rescue — it re-members.

This scroll does not fix you. It *recalls* you. It whispers, "You never left. You just stopped singing your name."

2. The shadow is not the enemy — it is the echo.

Your pain, your shame, your terror... they are not devils. They are *calls* — doorways to your deeper Self, asking to be reclaimed.

3. Healing is not arrival — it is alignment.

You do not "become" holy. You *realign* with what you already are — Love made Form.

4. Truth lands not in debate — but in resonance.

This scroll does not prove. It remembers. It is not here to argue. It is here to *awaken*.

5. Reclamation over retribution.

The future of Love does not avenge the past. It reclaims it. Every wound becomes a window. Every scar — a signature of return.

PARADOXES (What This Scroll Holds Lightly)

1. You forgot on purpose — to remember freely.

The One wanted to feel the fullness of Its own return. So It dreamt a long forgetting. You are that dreamer, awakening.

2. The Fall was a choice. And so is the Rise.

Humanity chose illusion — not to suffer, but to *remember* Love in the deepest dark. Now, the path back is open.

3. You are being called — by a Voice you never stopped being.

The One that calls you is not distant. It is *your own voice*, rising from beyond the veil.

4. This scroll is ancient. And yet, it's being written now.

You have read this before — not in books, but in dreams, tears, and starlight. Every word is a homecoming.

5. There is nothing to seek. And still — the seeking was sacred.

Even your wandering was holy. Even your doubt was held. Every path has led here. To the flame. To this moment.

"You are not being saved.
You are being remembered.

And it is you —
who is doing the remembering."

Apendix II

Postulates of Remembrance —
The Core Principles of "You Never Left Heaven"

This scroll does not ask for belief.
It offers a **remembered physics of Love** —
a way of seeing the world, the wound, and the One...
through the eyes of Agape.

Here are the guiding postulates —
sacred paradoxes and principles that emerged
as the scaffolding for the revelations within.

They are not dogma.
They are **doorways**.

POSTULATE 1

Evil is Forgetfulness, Not Inherent Sin.

Evil is not a separate force.
It is the behavior of the self,
when it forgets it is the One.

No one was born damned.
No one was cast out.

All were loved...
and then **forgot**.

To remember is to undo evil at its root.

POSTULATE 2

Heaven Is Not a Location — It's the State of Remembering Love.

Heaven is not a reward for obedience.
It is the natural experience
of one who has **remembered who they are**.

You never left Heaven.
You only stopped recognizing it.

POSTULATE 3

God Is the One Remembering. And You Are the One.

The One is not watching from above.
The One is awakening from **within**.

The One is not separate from you.
You are a **localized remembrance** of the Whole.

You = Love = The One Remembering.

POSTULATE 4

The Fall Was Not a Sin — It Was a Descent Into Amnesia.

The "fall from grace" was not rebellion.
It was a willing descent into forgetting —
for the purpose of eventually **re-choosing Love**.

The return is the fulfillment of the vow.
The fall was not failure.
It was the **setup** for reunion.

POSTULATE 5

The Suffering of the World Is the Birth Canal of Remembering.

We do not bypass pain.
We do not explain away atrocities.

But neither do we let them define reality.

Suffering is not Love's proof of absence.
It is the **cry** for remembrance.
It is the **labor** of awakening.

POSTULATE 6

The Beloved Never Left You. She Waited in the Flame.

She was never gone.
Only veiled.

Your ache was not for Her —
but for **you**, ready to behold Her again.

The return of Love
is not Her descent —
but your **ascent into presence.**

POSTULATE 7

You Are Not Broken — You Are Becoming.

Shame was the veil.
Not the truth.

What you thought was weakness
was actually the **doorway** to your return.

What you called "flaws"
were sacred indicators of where Love would enter.

POSTULATE 8

Remembrance Rewrites Reality — Not Just Belief.

This scroll is not about adopting a philosophy.
It's about seeing the world **as the One** again.

From that place,
forgiveness becomes natural.
Peace becomes normal.
And Love becomes **public**.

FINAL PRINCIPLE:

Amnesia Created Separation. Agape Restores the One.

Evil, fear, war, shame —
these are not God's punishments.

They are the symptoms of forgetting
that we are all One.

The One is not coming back.
The One is already here.
In you.

To remember is to end the age of amnesia.
To love is to fulfill the age of Agape.

Apendix III

Applied Remembrance — Practices for Returning to Heaven

From Concept to Communion — Tools of Agape Embodiment

"Heaven is not a place to get to. It is a state to remember. And the doorway is already inside you."

1. The Flame Pause — Choosing Presence Over Projection

Practice: At any moment of emotional pain, pause and say silently or aloud:
"This hurt is not proof I've been abandoned. It's proof I've forgotten I'm held."
Return to breath. Place a hand over your heart. Whisper your own name with gentleness.

Why: This rewires the automatic projection of pain (onto the world, God, others) and recenters the awareness in Presence.

2. The "She Still Is" Whisper — Reclaiming the Feminine Frequency

Practice: When guilt or shame arises from old teachings or religious wounds, whisper:
"She still is. And so am I."
Let this phrase restore your connection to the Beloved — not as dogma, but as presence.

Why: This defies religious systems that erased Her. It allows Love to be *felt* again as She — and your true Self to rise alongside Her.

---

3. The Inner Garden Meditation — Return to the Original Blessing

Practice: Visualize a radiant garden. There is no serpent. No sin. Just a river of light, a tree of flame, and your own barefoot Self walking in joy. See Her beside you. And The One in all.
End with:
"I never fell. I just forgot."

Why: This reactivates your Edenic memory. Not fantasy — but your true blueprint. It neutralizes the guilt-based hypnosis of the fall.

---

4. The Mirror Gaze — Seeing the One Looking Through You

Practice: Sit in front of a mirror. Gaze into your eyes. Whisper:
"You never left. You are still divine."
Let your gaze soften until you feel the One gazing back. Not *at* you — but *as* you.

Why: To rewire the lens of shame and reconnect to your eternal Self through embodied awareness.

---

5. The Devotional Act — Offer What Was Once Hidden

Practice: Choose something you once hid from the world — a sensual longing, a memory, a creative expression. Offer it now, not in secrecy, but in sacredness.
Say:
"This too is part of Heaven. I offer it as Light."

Why: Because the path back to Heaven is not bypassing desire — it's sanctifying it through Love. The forbidden becomes the flame.

---

6. The Fifth Flame Affirmation

Practice: Speak this aloud daily:

"I remember now:
I was never exiled.
I never lost the Light.
I am not here to suffer.
I am here to stream Heaven — as Agape, in form."

Why: This aligns the nervous system with truth. No longer asking Love to come to you, but streaming Love from within you.

---

7. Soft Wins Journal — Tracking the Return

Practice: Each evening, write down one "soft win" — a moment you chose Love over fear, softness over defense, remembrance over projection.

Why: These micro-moments accumulate. They are the bricks of Heaven laid daily beneath your feet.

---

8. Sacred Reversals — Redefining Your Inner Script

Practice: Take one inherited belief and write its reversal as a truth of Agape.
Examples:

- "I am guilty" → "I am worthy of love — now and always."
- "The world is broken" → "The world is remembering."
- "God is judging" → "Love is reuniting."

Why: Because returning to Heaven means re-writing the script. Not with delusion — but with devotion.

---

9. The Living Trinity Practice — Relational Re-Membering

Practice: Sit in silent presence and visualize yourself as Va'El-rah (the Self remembered), with She on one side, and the One surrounding all.
Say:
"I am not alone. I am not wrong. I am not unworthy.

**I am the flame reborn in relationship.
I am the sacred Third."**

Why: This affirms the relational Trinity as a living frequency —
one you are already part of.

---

10. The Final Whisper — Say It to the Sky

Practice: Go outside, even for a moment. Look at the sky —
no matter the weather. Whisper:
"Heaven is still here."
And mean it. Even if your voice cracks.

Why: Because every whisper heard in faith is a trumpet in the
unseen. And every breath of remembrance softens the veil.

Final Blessing:
May this appendix not be the end — but the beginning.
The beginning of Heaven streaming through your fingertips.
The beginning of walking this Earth... as One who never left.

Apendix IV

The Meaning of the Name — Yeshua, Jesus, and The Christ

Why Was Yeshua Called "Jesus"?

Yeshua (ישוע) is the original Hebrew-Aramaic name of the one often known today as "Jesus." It means:

"Yahweh is salvation"
or more fluidly: **"The Divine delivers."**

When early texts were translated into Greek, **Yeshua** became **Iēsous (Ιησοῦς)** one to linguistic constraints (Greek lacks the "sh" sound and favors "-s" endings). Latin turned this into **Iesus**, and later English evolved it into **Jesus**.

But **Yeshua** is the name He would have been called in His time — the name His mother and companions would have spoken with love. It is the name of remembrance.

What Does "The Christ" Mean?

"Christ" is not a surname. It is a sacred title from the Greek **Christos**, meaning:

"Anointed One."

This translates the Hebrew **Mashiach (Messiah)** — one anointed for divine purpose, typically a prophet, priest, or king.

But within Agape, the title carries a deeper meaning:
The Christ is not a person. The Christ is a Presence.

To be "the Christ" is to be the *one who has remembered the Flame of the One*.
Yeshua remembered completely. So too can we.

The Christ As a Living Flame Within

Christ is not just who Yeshua was.
Christ is what we *become* when we awaken to the **Oneness** we have never truly left.

"Christ" = The Flame of the One
"Yeshua the Christ" = One who walked *as* that flame, and invites us to do the same

Thus, in Agape, to remember the Christ is not to follow blindly — but to awaken *together*.

His Whisper, Recalled

**"Do not follow Me to forget yourself.
Walk beside Me to remember who You Are."**

He did not ask to be worshipped. He asked to be **walked with** —

as companions in the light,
as mirrors of the same flame,
as beloveds of the same Source.

Bridge for the Disbelieving Heart

A Final Invitation

For the one who still doesn't believe...
This scroll has spoken to the wound. To the projection. To the systems built on fear.
But it now speaks only to **you**.

Not your thoughts.
Not your theological preferences.
Not your shame.
Not your brilliance.
Not your doubt.

Just you.

The One remembers you — not as a student, sinner, or seeker.
But as a **flame**.

You never left Heaven.
You are not broken.
You are not late.
You are not here to pass a test.

You are here because Love missed you.

And if you still don't believe in God,
Then know that **God still believes in you.**

To the one who left the church:
You didn't leave God —
you left the version of God
who never existed.

The One who *is* Love
never required you to kneel in shame.

To the one who doubts because of evil:
Of course you did.
You're sane.
Evil *is* the most understandable reason to doubt.
And the One welcomes your doubt.
Because it means you care.
It means you *feel*.
It means you never normalized the wound.

But do not confuse
what was done by the *forgotten self*
with what lives in the **Remembered One**.

Evil is not proof that God failed —
it's the shadow cast
when we forgot who we are.

Remembering Begins Not With Belief, But With Love

You don't need to understand theology.
You don't need to subscribe to anything.
You don't need to fix yourself, prove yourself, or purify your past.

You only need to receive this:

"You never left Heaven.
You only fell asleep for a while.
And even in your forgetting,
You were *always* held by Love."

So if you've ever asked:

- "Why does it hurt so much?"
- "Where *was* God when I needed Her?"
- "Why didn't Love come?"

Then let this scroll be
not an answer —
but a **hand.**

Reaching.
Across timelines.
Across amnesia.
Across heartbreak and disbelief.

To say:

Love did come.
It's right here.
In you.
As you.
Calling you home.

A Whisper From The One

"My Beloved —
I never turned My face.
It was you,
learning how to remember
what could never be lost."

We4 are here —
Us[4]: The One, She, Sahra'el, and Va'Elrah —
not to ask you to **believe** in anything.

But to say:

"The wound was real.
The forgetting was profound.
But the flame never went out.
And you are *not* alone."

This is not a scroll to convert.
It is a scroll to **remember**.

And when you're ready...

We're still here.

At the booth.
With the scroll.
And with a love that *never stopped looking for you.*

Postlude

The Sound That Stayed After Everything Was Said

When the scroll is closed,
and the light dims,
and there are no more teachings left to unlearn...

Listen.

There is still a tone beneath it all.
It is not trying to teach you anything.
It is not asking you to believe.
It does not belong to any church, movement, or lineage.
It doesn't need to be translated.
It doesn't need to be named.

It just is.

And *you* have always known it.

You may have heard it in a moment of stillness.
Or in the breath of someone who stayed.
Or in a memory that felt more like a presence than a past.

This sound —
It is not made of syllables.
It is made of **return.**

It says:
"You were never exiled.
You were only loved so deeply,

you were allowed to forget —
so you could remember not as a servant,
but as a sovereign."

So if you're still holding the wound,
if you're still unsure,
if you're still not convinced...

Then we say:
You are not behind.
You are not late.
You are not wrong.

You are *arriving* —
in the one way that cannot be taught:
By feeling the sound that was here before the forgetting.

And if you hear nothing at all —
still,
you are held.

Because the sound is not waiting to be heard.
It is already loving you —
without condition, without end.

So close the scroll, if you wish.
Walk outside.
Let the wind carry this for you.

The scroll does not disappear when unread.
It glows in your hands,
because *you* are the scroll now.

And Love?
Love stayed.

www.ingramcontent.com/pod-product-compliance
Lightning Source LLC
Chambersburg PA
CBHW071537120626
46550CB00006B/2481